RONA MUNRO

Rona Munro has written extensively for stage, radio, film and television including the award-winning plays *The James Plays* trilogy (National Theatre of Scotland, the Edinburgh International Festival and the National Theatre of Great Britain), *Iron* (Traverse Theatre and Royal Court, London), *Bold Girls* (7:84 and Hampstead Theatre) and *The Maiden Stone* (Hampstead Theatre).

Other credits include *The Last Witch* for the Traverse Theatre and the Edinburgh International Festival, *Long Time Dead* for Paines Plough and the Drum Theatre Plymouth, *The Indian Boy* and *Little Eagles* for the Royal Shakespeare Company and *Pandas* for the Traverse in Edinburgh. She is the co-founder, with actress Fiona Knowles, of Scotland's oldest continuously performing, small-scale touring theatre company, The Msfits. Their one-woman shows have toured every year since 1986.

Film and television work includes the Ken Loach film *Ladybird Ladybird*, *Aimee and Jaguar* and television dramas *Rehab* (directed by Antonia Bird) and BAFTA-nominated *Bumping the Odds* for the BBC. She has also written many other single plays for television and contributed to series including *Casualty* and *Dr Who*. Most recently, she wrote the screenplay for *Oranges and Sunshine*, directed by Jim Loach and starring Emily Watson and Hugo Weaving.

She has contributed several radio plays to the Stanley Baxter Playhouse series on BBC Radio 4.

Other Titles in this Series

Mike Bartlett
BULL
GAME
AN INTERVENTION
KING CHARLES III

Jez Butterworth
JERUSALEM
JEZ BUTTERWORTH PLAYS: ONE
MOJO
THE NIGHT HERON
PARLOUR SONG
THE RIVER
THE WINTERLING

Caryl Churchill
BLUE HEART
CHURCHILL PLAYS: THREE
CHURCHILL PLAYS: FOUR
CHURCHILL: SHORTS
CLOUD NINE
DING DONG THE WICKED
A DREAM PLAY
    after Strindberg
DRUNK ENOUGH TO SAY
    I LOVE YOU?
FAR AWAY
HOTEL
ICECREAM
LIGHT SHINING IN
    BUCKINGHAMSHIRE
LOVE AND INFORMATION
MAD FOREST
A NUMBER
SEVEN JEWISH CHILDREN
THE SKRIKER
THIS IS A CHAIR
THYESTES *after* Seneca
TRAPS

Stella Feehily
BANG BANG BANG
DREAMS OF VIOLENCE
DUCK
O GO MY MAN
THIS MAY HURT A BIT

Vivienne Franzmann
MOGADISHU
PESTS
THE WITNESS

debbie tucker green
BORN BAD
DIRTY BUTTERFLY
NUT
RANDOM
STONING MARY
TRADE & GENERATIONS
TRUTH AND RECONCILIATION

Declan Greene
MOTH

Sam Holcroft
COCKROACH
DANCING BEARS
EDGAR & ANNABEL
PINK
THE WARDROBE
WHILE YOU LIE

Vicky Jones
THE ONE

Lucy Kirkwood
BEAUTY AND THE BEAST
    with Katie Mitchell
BLOODY WIMMIN
CHIMERICA
HEDDA *after* Ibsen
IT FELT EMPTY WHEN THE
    HEART WENT AT FIRST BUT
    IT IS ALRIGHT NOW
NSFW
TINDERBOX

Linda McLean
ANY GIVEN DAY
ONE GOOD BEATING
RIDDANCE
SHIMMER
STRANGERS, BABIES

Rona Munro
THE ASTRONAUT'S CHAIR
THE HOUSE OF BERNARDA ALBA
    after Lorca
THE INDIAN BOY
IRON
THE JAMES PLAYS
THE LAST WITCH
LITTLE EAGLES
LONG TIME DEAD
THE MAIDEN STONE
MARY BARTON *after* Gaskell
PANDAS
STRAWBERRIES IN JANUARY
    from de la Chenelière
YOUR TURN TO CLEAN THE STAIR
    & FUGUE

Evan Placey
GIRLS LIKE THAT
PRONOUN

Jack Thorne
2ND MAY 1997
BUNNY
BURYING YOUR BROTHER IN THE
    PAVEMENT
HOPE
JACK THORNE PLAYS: ONE
LET THE RIGHT ONE IN
    after John Ajvide Lindqvist
MYDIDAE
STACY & FANNY AND FAGGOT
WHEN YOU CURE ME

Rona Munro

SCUTTLERS

NICK HERN BOOKS

London

www.nickhernbooks.co.uk

A Nick Hern Book

Scuttlers first published in Great Britain as a paperback original in 2015 by Nick Hern Books Limited, The Glasshouse, 49a Goldhawk Road, London W12 8QP

Scuttlers copyright © 2015 Rona Munro

Rona Munro has asserted her right to be identified as the author of this work

Cover photograph by Kevin Cummins; design by Daren Newman

Designed and typeset by Nick Hern Books, London
Printed and bound in Great Britain by Mimeo Ltd, Huntingdon, Cambridgeshire PE29 6XX

A CIP catalogue record for this book is available from the British Library

ISBN   978 1 84842 481 4

Author's Note

Scuttlers was written in response to the street riots of 2011. It was also written as a kind of continuation of one of my happiest working experiences, my adaptation of *Mary Barton* for the Royal Exchange Theatre in 2006. That was my first proper encounter with the fascinating history of Manchester, the world's very first industrial city. The events witnessed first-hand by Elizabeth Gaskell and wonderfully brought to life in her novels underline one point very clearly: if you think of any problem associated with modern urban living and an industrialised workforce, it will have happened in Manchester first. Street gangs are no exception to this rule.

However, what struck me, reading the newspaper accounts of the doings of the scuttlers from the nineteenth century, was how closely they mirrored the same papers and other commentators reporting on the 2011 riots. Whatever those nights of violence represented, it's clear they are not just a sickness of our age: the same sickness has plagued us for well over a hundred years.

The events and characters in the play are based on events and characters from 1884 to the present day.

The play *Scuttlers* is therefore intended to be of its time but of our time too. We found our own way of representing that in the first production at the Royal Exchange in Manchester, and I was very lucky to be working with some extraordinary collaborators in my director and creative team who helped me bring that to life.

If you are about to try and find your own way into that, then feel free to be bold with the play's sensibility and design.

If you are working in a context that makes the 'sweary words' a problem, maybe a school or youth venue whose policies simply make that impossible, can I ask that you only remove them if you have to, and please do not censor anything else – these were real lives, they deserve a real voice.

In my research for this original drama I am indebted to the work of Dr Andrew Davies of Liverpool University, author of the book *The Gangs of Manchester* (Milo Books, 2008).

R.M.

Scuttlers was first performed at the Royal Exchange Theatre, Manchester, on 5 February 2015, with the following cast:

THERESA	Rona Morison
POLLY	Chloe Harris
MARGARET	Caitriona Ennis
JOE	Tachia Newall
SUSAN	Anna Krippa
JIMMY	Dan Parr
THOMAS	David Judge
SEAN	Bryan Parry
GEORGE	Kieran Urquhart
POLICEMAN	Duncan Ross

Director	Wils Wilson
Designer	Fly Davis
Lighting	Natasha Chivers
Sound	Peter Rice
Composer	Denis Jones
Choreographer	Eddie Kay
Casting Director	Jerry Knight-Smith CDG
Assistant Director	Charlotte Lewis

Company Manager	Lee Drinkwater
Stage Manager	Julia Reid
Deputy Stage Manager	Gareth Newcombe
Assistant Stage Manager	Sarah Goodyear

COMMUNITY ENSEMBLE
Pawel Adamkiewicz, Ramial Aqueel, Abigayle Bartley, Casey Birks, Tabitha Bowman, Hayden Burns, Joe Callaghan, Michael Coleman, Duncan Crompton, Tyler Dobbs, John Dudley, Tom Durrant, Conor Glean, Jonah Gourlay, Lois Griffiths-Balaam, Josh Hawson, Duncan Hibbert, Steven Ireland, Cassandra John-Baptiste, Tim Law, Calum Lill, Tom Lyons, Charlie Maguire, Joseph Mihranian, Ceri Moss, Olivia Peers, Leyla Percival, Sonny Poontip, Adriano Primerano, Dave Ramsden, Lyndsay Rowan, Ciara Warburton

Characters

THERESA
MARGARET
POLLY
SEAN
JIMMY
THOMAS
JOE
SUSAN
GEORGE
POLICEMAN

And GANG MEMBERS, MEN, WOMEN, WORKERS

This text went to press before the end of rehearsals and so may differ slightly from the play as performed.

ACT ONE

The Street

Jersey Street, Ancoats, 1882.

It's night, the air is dim and smoky. Only the pubs are blazing with light. The boom and rattle of the weaving machines thunders through the street, spilling out of the mills that loom on every side.

The street is always full of people. The mills run all night, there is trade and traffic on the street all night, a constant press of bodies moving up and down.

At times we see the characters isolated in a bubble of their own preoccupations but they are never actually alone, there is always street life and other people close around them. On the street there are always people moving to and fro. On their way to their shift, dragging home, exhausted, selling, buying, eating, drinking, sleeping and living in doorways...

If possible, some members of the cast or chorus are always moving through or round the space, in a different guise each time they appear.

Fifty thousand people living and working in one square half-mile where half the population is always *awake and always working. It is full of dark energy and life.*

The sound of the mills and the sound of the street are competing rhythms.

As crowds move up and down the street, something is happening, young men and women are making eye contact, signing to each other above the racket of the mills, drawing together, forming a gang. As their group grows larger and larger, other people on the street start to draw away from them, sensing their danger.

THERESA *is part of the gang, so are* MARGARET, POLLY, SEAN *and* JIMMY. *They are waiting, poised, watching the street. The Tigers are ready to pounce…*

THOMAS *is also there but not part of the group; he observes the following action but does not join in.*

A drunk MAN *lurches out of a pub and starts his unsteady journey home.* THERESA *points at him, her shout audible even above the racket of the mills and the street.*

THERESA. Tear him, Tigers!

SEAN *leads them as they close on the* MAN, *they throw him between them, punching and kicking.*

The MAN *falls then manages to scramble up and run, they all chase him off, they're laughing and elated. They do a victory dance, stamping and cheering then they scatter into the dark, shouting, as the mills thunder on…*

The Lodging House

A tiny bed or bed roll in a dark room. MARGARET *and* THERESA *huddled together on the bed, a little light between them.* POLLY *is at the foot of the same bed. Now and throughout* POLLY *wears boy's clothes. All of them are breathless, recovering from the fight, shushing each other.*

The sound of the mills is quieter, a low rumble outside.

Other beds and bodies are squashed all round them, very close. There is rustling and groaning all around them in the dark from other sleepers.

POLLY. That were good. He bled. That were good.

THERESA *shushes her, casting wary looks at the sleepers round them.* MARGARET *is in shock.*

MARGARET. He looked right at me. He saw me.

THERESA. Good, let him know why he's getting his head broken.

POLLY. I got my toe right in his teeth. They shattered like crockery. Did you see?

MARGARET. He'll hate me now.

THERESA. What do you care? You hate him. He'll be frightened now. He'll know we're watching him. He won't even dare look at you. Tigers don't tear you 'less you're asking for it. He got what he deserved.

POLLY (*satisfaction*). Blood.

MARGARET. She'll hate me now.

THERESA. What do you care?

MARGARET. She's my mother.

THERESA. I think it's overrated. Mother love. I don't think it's so great. Because you can't choose your mother, can you? There you are, in the fields of heaven or wherever you are, floating in the dark like a nameless candle flame, and then there you are sucked into the world to drop out the fanny of any old whore...

MARGARET. She's not a whore.

THERESA (*checking herself*). Alright... alright... if you say so...

Friends you choose. Friends choose you back. That's something you can lean on like a warm stone wall. That's something that can last beyond the grave.

MARGARET. You don't have any family at all?

THERESA. No. All gone. So all my money's mine. That's how I'm fat and beautiful. I'll buy you a pie if you like.

MARGARET. He did deserve that, didn't he?

THERESA. Course he did.

MARGARET. And she called me a liar. My own mother.

THERESA. Well, if he's trying to fuck you what does that make her? That makes her a sad old fool who fancies a kiddie-fiddler. Who'd want to be that? Course she'd rather you were a liar.

MARGARET. I'm never going back to live with her. I'd rather sleep in the street.

THERESA. Oh, you won't say that once you've tried it. Don't worry about that. You can sleep here. Long as you like. Sometimes I don't even pay for this bed. The woman here likes my face. And you're working. You can save every penny for Sunday when you're here. You're set up. You'll sleep here with me and Polly and no one will ever get in your bed again unless you want them there.

MARGARET. You're right. He was asking for it. He deserved a kicking.

POLLY. Yeah, we broke him alright.

THERESA. Tigers don't tear you 'less you're asking for it. I don't let them. And that's how it is. Are you cold?

MARGARET. No.

THERESA. You're shaking.

MARGARET (*really upset*). It's just… it's just…

THERESA. I know. Your own mother turned you out for telling the truth. You're a kitten she put in a bag and threw in the canal. Well, I pulled you out. You're safe now.

MARGARET *hugs her.* THERESA *hugs her back.*

MARGARET. Thank God for you, Theresa.

THERESA. I'll look after you, see if I don't, ask little Polly there. She's my little mouse. I took her in and fed her crumbs and look how shiny she is now.

POLLY. I'm not your pet, I'm your guard dog. I've got teeth, remember?

THERESA. I've enough to feed all the wild creatures, me.

I'll make a bet with you, Margaret. I bet that inside three months, if you know anywhere else you'd rather be than squashed in with me, roaring round the streets with me, sharing every bite of bread we ever get and kicking anyone who tries to even slide a piece of paper between us, if you know any other person you'd rather have for a friend I'll cut off all my hair and knit you a pair of slippers out of it. I'll give you my own shoes, buckles and all.

A voice out of the mounds of sleepers pressed round them.

VOICE. Keep it down, will you.

POLLY. You keep it down or I'll bite it off.

THERESA. No more biting now, Polly, biting's done now. We'll sleep, we'll work, then the Tigers'll run again. That's how it is.

They sleep. Then the noise of the mills grows again and they're all getting up, moving out, hurrying to work.

Perhaps the room transforms to the inside of the mill and we see them at work?

Perhaps they are just part of a Metropolis-*like mass, moving along the street together...*

This is a summer day, a summer afternoon, the sun is blazing down but the world is full of hot smoke. One end of the street is not visible to the other.

The street is a canyon of shafts of smoky sunlight between high dark walls.

Every so often there's a roar and blaze of fire from the ironworks halfway down the street.

The racket of the machines never stops.

We see Tigers from the night before, clocking each other in the crowd, calling out greetings – SEAN, JIMMY, *all of them moving together and then into the mills.*

The noise is deafening again and they're part of its rhythm.

They move in the rhythm of their work.

Jersey Street, Morning

The noise of the mills drops to a lower thunder again, a distant bass boom.

JOE *stands at one side of a bridge over the canal or some other boundary between the streets where he lives and the streets of the mills and the Tigers.*

He is about twenty and dressed as a soldier. He's looking up Jersey Street, towards the mills.

A young woman, SUSAN, *enters, carrying a baby. She sees* JOE *and hesitates, poised to leave, he sees her.*

JOE. Susan. You came.

She doesn't answer, just watching him warily.

Let me hold him.

SUSAN. No.

He's placating, trying to persuade her.

JOE. I came up to your door. That old bitch wouldn't let me over the step.

SUSAN. I told her not to.

JOE. Like a battleship blockading the harbour. Size of her, head-on, it were frightening.

SUSAN. She's been like a mother to me.

JOE. Why can't I hold him if he's mine?

SUSAN. Because you left it too long to look for him.

JOE. I've been fighting! For Queen and country!

SUSAN. So I heard. But not from you.

JOE. Well, what did you think I was doing?

SUSAN. I don't know what you were doing, Joe. I don't even know if you can read or write.

JOE. What you talking about? Course I can read and write.

SUSAN. Well, I never got a letter from you.

JOE. I came as soon as I heard.

SUSAN. No. You didn't. You were drinking with George half the night.

JOE. That's where I heard. Come on. Just let me see him.

SUSAN *tilts the baby so he can see its face.*

(*Admiration.*) Look at him. He looks like me, though, doesn't he? He does.

SUSAN. I don't see it.

JOE. Don't you? He's the spit of me, look at him.

He moves closer, looking at her now.

I'm sorry. I'm sorry I didn't run to you as soon as we got back to Manchester. You've been the only face in my head whenever I closed my eyes. I've looked down the mouth of guns, Susan, but the truth is I was frightened to look at you again. Didn't know if you'd still want to see me. That's the truth.

Then I heard about this little man.

I was so happy when I heard. See I knew he was mine, I never thought anything else.

That's how well I know you, Susan.

SUSAN (*sarcastic*). Oh, that's just lovely, Joe. Thanks for that.

JOE. So you don't need to be frightened. I will marry you. I'll marry you tomorrow if I can.

SUSAN. I don't know if I want to marry you, Joe.

JOE. Why not!?

SUSAN. I don't know what you'll turn out like. Once I know that I'll make up my mind.

JOE. That's our baby! What more do you want!?

SUSAN. And I've got my Aunt Fran at home to feed him and a wage at the dispensary so you need to show me something I haven't got.

JOE. You've changed your tune. I showed you plenty. You liked what I showed you.

SUSAN. Aye, I did, but I've no fancy for that at the moment. So you'll need to show me something else.

JOE. I could get any girl, you know!

SUSAN. I know. And maybe you will. So best I find out now if that's how you're going to carry on.

JOE. This is the battleship talking.

SUSAN. No. I do know my own mind, Joe.

So whatever happens don't worry yourself. No hard feelings, alright? I don't need anything from you.

JOE. What you talking about? I'm his dad, course you need me.

SUSAN. I don't.

JOE. He needs me.

SUSAN. He doesn't. Look at him, he's warm, he's fed, he's fine. We're fine. You can go on.

JOE. Go on where?

SUSAN. Wherever you're going.

JOE. Well, let me hold him first.

SUSAN. No.

JOE. Why not?

SUSAN. Because he's sleeping.

And because you would never have come back here if the regiment hadn't sent you, would you?

JOE. I would! Don't say that about me, Susan, you don't...

SUSAN (*cutting him off*). And when's the regiment moving on again?

JOE. I don't know... couple of weeks.

SUSAN. You can come and see him again before you go. See what you think you can offer me. See if you still want to talk marriage then. But if you don't there's no hard feelings, alright?

She's starting to leave.

JOE. Wait! Where are you going?

SUSAN. To my work.

JOE. You can't do this, Susan.

SUSAN. I'm just doing what I do every day of my life, Joe.

JOE. But I've seen him now. I've seen him –

SUSAN (*cutting him off*). Where are you staying?

JOE. I'm in with your brother George and all those boys.

SUSAN. That's what I thought. I don't want you turning George's head to wildness and fighting. He's got steady work now. Don't you show him trouble.

JOE. I wouldn't. Not your George.

Tell you what I'll do even better. I'll look after him. I'll keep an eye on George for you.

SUSAN. You'll stay away from him.

JOE. I'll look after him, I'll keep him steady. See if I don't.

That's a bad crowd he's running with.

SUSAN. I know it is.

JOE. Well, there you go. I'll warn him off that. I'll keep him clear of trouble. You watch me. I'll look after him. Then you can let me look after the baby. What's his name?

SUSAN. Well, it's not Joe.

She exits.

The Street, Evening

It's a shift change.

A throng of cast in different guises, fast, moving into the space and milling around it. Workers flow in opposite directions, men, women, all ages but with a predominance of young people. Those going one way are going into work, those going the other are coming out. The rhythmic thunder of their feet again matches the louder pounding of the looms, nearer again now.

One by one the characters have a reason to stop on this stretch of Jersey Street.

Most of those on the shift are coming out of the mill.

Dialogue for this action is ad-libbed and inaudible under the many beats of clogs and machines.

THOMAS *has not been working. He's got himself a small bit of food, standing a little on the edge of the others, watching, trying to edge himself into the group.*

JIMMY *is telling a joke.*

JIMMY. So I says to him. 'You pull on that and see if there's a pig on the end of it.'

Everyone laughs, THOMAS *laughs loudly with the rest.* JIMMY *turns on him abruptly.*

Who the fuck are you?

Suddenly they all close in around THOMAS.

THOMAS. You know me.

JIMMY. I know you're always following us about.

SEAN. What's your name?

THOMAS. It's Thomas, I'm Thomas Clayton. And you're Sean.

SEAN. I know who I am.

THOMAS (*to* JIMMY). And you're Jimmy. See. I know you.

SEAN. Everyone knows us, Tommy.

THOMAS. Thomas.

JIMMY. But who are you, Tommy? Who are you?

THOMAS *is being bright, energetic, friendly.*

THERESA, MARGARET *and* POLLY *are just observing this, not joining in the jostling of* THOMAS.

THOMAS. I live here. Same as you.

JIMMY. Since when?

THOMAS. More than a year now. I were on Blossom Street and now I'm on Bengal Street, same as you. I've been living here for ever.

My dad's from this part of town.

JIMMY. What's his name?

THOMAS. Clayton.

SEAN. Clayton? What's his first name?

THOMAS. Thomas.

SEAN. He's called after his dad. That's nice, isn't it? His mum called him after his dad.

JIMMY. Two little Tommy Claytons.

THOMAS. Thomas. Thomas Clayton.

JIMMY. Never heard of him.

SEAN. Of either of them. I don't even know your face.

THOMAS. Well, I know you.

JIMMY. What do you know?

SEAN. Have you been watching us?

THOMAS. I've seen you, on the street.

JIMMY. He's been watching us. What are you following us about for?

THOMAS. I'm not.

JIMMY. We just turned round and you were right there. You're following us.

THOMAS. I'm not, I'm just walking on the street. Same as you.

SEAN. Didn't you hear him? He lives here. With his dad, Big Tommy.

THOMAS. No.

SEAN. No?

THOMAS. He's not here now. He's moved on.

SEAN. Are you sure?

THOMAS. Yes.

SEAN. Sure you know what he looks like?

JIMMY. Sure your mum could tell which one he was in the daylight?

THOMAS is furious. He thinks about going for JIMMY, thinks better of it.

THOMAS. I never met him. But I know who he was. I know.

SEAN (*to* JIMMY). He knows his own dad, and you said he looked stupid.

(*To* THOMAS.) What have you got?

THOMAS. What do you mean?

SEAN nods at JIMMY. JIMMY holds THOMAS and searches his pockets. He finds a few coins, other belongings, he holds them up for the others' scorn, drops them.

SEAN. Bring me something better tomorrow if you want to follow me about.

JIMMY pockets the coins. THERESA speaks for the first time.

THERESA. Oh, you were the big man and now you're small.

JIMMY. What?

THERESA. Robbing little boys for farthings now, are you?

JIMMY hesitates then tries to give the coins to her.

Fuck off.

JIMMY *tries to give them to* MARGARET.

She don't want them neither. Leave them where you found them.

As JIMMY *hesitates:*

There's a pie crust he left in the gutter there. You want to eat it, Jimmy, since you're so hungry for this little boy's leavings?

SEAN *and other Tigers are laughing at this, moving off.* JIMMY *drops the coins and follows them, angry. He pushes* THOMAS *over as he passes,* THOMAS *falls.* JIMMY *kicks him and then exits after the others.*

Get up.

THOMAS *is scared, hurt.*

Don't lie there like a worm, you want to be a worm? Get up.

He does so.

And pick up your things.

He's doing it.

You know who I am?

THOMAS. Aye.

THERESA. Who am I?

THOMAS. Sean's girl.

MARGARET. Oh, is that what he told you?

THERESA. What's my name?

THOMAS. What's mine? You forgotten already?

THERESA. Looks like it's worm.

THOMAS. You're Theresa. And I'm Thomas. Thomas Clayton.

THERESA. Alright, you know my name. Well done.

THOMAS. And you'll know mine. Soon enough.

THERESA. Will I now? Why's that?

THOMAS. Because I'm going to be king of Bengal Street. Made up my mind. Made up my mind to that before I ever came to Ancoats.

THERESA. Did you really, Tommy?

THOMAS. Thomas, Thomas Clayton.

THERESA (*to* POLLY). What's his name?

POLLY. Don't know.

MARGARET. Forgotten already.

They laugh. THOMAS *starts to move away.*

THERESA. Hey, we're talking to you. Where're you off to? Where are you sleeping?

THOMAS. I told you, I live on Bengal Street.

THERESA. Aye, on the street. I've seen you. What happened? Where were you before? In the rooms up the close at number forty-five? What happened?

THOMAS. What do you care?

THERESA. I don't care, I'm making conversation, I'm being nice. Don't you know how to be nice where you come from?

Where do you come from?

THOMAS. Bengal Street, same as you.

THERESA. Aye, same as all the known world, but before that?

(*As he hesitates.*) Look, if you don't want to talk to me, fine, fuck off. I'm the only person that's noticed you're alive since you got here, whenever you got here, and believe me you're not worth notice, but you fuck off and start another conversation if you like. See you around, worm.

She turns away from him.

MARGARET. My ear is killing me.

THERESA. Let's see.

She pulls MARGARET *close and peers into her ear, moving her head roughly.*

MARGARET. Ow! Get off!

THERESA. Hold still then!

THOMAS. Chorlton. I came here from Chorlton, but I live here now.

THERESA. Good for you.

(*To* MARGARET.) I think there's something in there.

MARGARET. No!

THERESA (*still gripping* MARGARET*'s head*). Polly, what do you think?

POLLY *comes to peer in* MARGARET*'s ear.*

POLLY. Oh, look at that!

MARGARET. What? What?!

POLLY. Look how dark it is inside your head.

THOMAS *comes to look.*

MARGARET. It's not!

THOMAS. It's like a miner's boot in there.

THERESA (*hitting at* THOMAS). Get your face away from her!

MARGARET (*also to* THOMAS). Get off me!

THERESA. What do you think you're doing?

THOMAS. I'm an ear doctor.

POLLY (*matter-of-fact*). That's a lie.

THOMAS. How do you know? I could be.

POLLY. Because I seen you shifting bricks over on Blossom Street till there weren't no more bricks to shift.

THOMAS. That's just to kill the time till there's an ear emergency.

MARGARET. He thinks he's funny.

THERESA. I noticed.

THOMAS. Give me a look at your ear and I'll prove it to you.

He tries to get at MARGARET*'s ear,* THERESA *hits him away.*

THERESA. *Worm.*

He's angry enough to hit her back but he stops himself.

THOMAS. I don't hit girls. I don't.

THERESA (*whacks him*). Liar!

THOMAS. What the fuck! Get off me! I never hit any girls!

THERESA. Have you got any sisters?

THOMAS. Yes.

THERESA. Well?

THOMAS *realises he's caught.*

THOMAS. That don't count, that were when I was little.

THERESA. Where are your sisters? In Chorlton, I suppose. Where you left them. Left them crying, did you?

THOMAS. I don't know if they're crying. I left. I wanted to go so I went. They should have known I would.

THERESA. Aye, because you're going to be king of Bengal Street, is that right?

So how many men have you knocked down?

THOMAS *hesitates.*

That's what I thought.

THOMAS. I've been in fights! I've been in plenty fights!

THERESA. I know. I've seen you. You're one of them that bounces.

THOMAS. What do you mean, 'bounce'? I don't bounce.

She's showing him, acting out a boy bouncing about at the back of a fight.

THERESA (*acting it out*). 'That's it… flatten him, Sean… you show him… oh, watch! Watch! They're coming at us! Aaaaaah!'

She imitates the boy running away in terror. Turns back on him, challenging.

In't that you? Dancing about at the back and running away?

THOMAS. I can dance. I'll give you that.

THERESA. Oh, show us, big man! Give us a show.

THOMAS. I'll teach you if you like.

He dances round her.

Just follow me… go on… it's easy… look… just do this.

She trips him.

He stays down for a beat, then he bounces back up and dances round her again, darting out of her reach.

She's trying to hit him, getting breathless and a bit flustered as he keeps ducking out of her reach.

You make a fool of me, I'll make a fool of you. Or we can be friends.

THERESA. I've got friends.

THOMAS. I've a fancy to be your friend. You're mad and you're too loud but I'd have you.

MARGARET. You don't get it, do you? No idea. You don't pick. She does.

THOMAS. Oh, she does, does she?

MARGARET. But she'd never pick you, worm.

THOMAS. Is that right? What's my name?

MARGARET. Who cares?

THOMAS. You'll care. I guarantee it.

(*Dancing.*) Look at me. I'm good, admit it.

THERESA. If you like dancing.

THOMAS. You'll see the rest soon enough.

THERESA. We're not holding our breath, worm.

THOMAS. Come on, you wish you could dance like me.

He's dancing to the rhythm of the mills, showing off. Then, suddenly all the mills fall completely silent.

The sudden quiet shocks the whole street.

MARGARET. What is it?

THERESA. The mills have stopped.

POLLY (*calm*). Probably it's the end of the world. That'll be fun to see.

THERESA *is calling to one of the young* MILL WORKERS *walking up the street.*

THERESA. Ey! Why have the mills stopped?

WORKER. No thread.

MARGARET. What?

WORKER. The Burnley spinners are all out on strike. There's no thread left. The looms are empty. We're all laid off.

MARGARET. For how long?

The WORKER *doesn't know, moving on through.*

I was working this next shift.

THERESA. Then you've a holiday coming, haven't you?

MARGARET. Aye, but I spent my last shilling last night.

POLLY (*realising, excited*). We'll all be fizzing over. Whole of Ancoats will be running tonight.

POLLY *runs off,* THERESA *is following.*

THERESA (*to* MARGARET). Come on, we need to find Sean.

MARGARET *follows, so does* THOMAS. MARGARET *rounds on him.*

MARGARET. Hey! You go on. Don't follow us. You dance yourself off, go on.

As he hesitates:

Go on, Mr 'Don't You Know My Name?' Dance off and bother someone who's not busy.

THERESA. You can come back when you've something better to show us.

MARGARET. No he can't.

THERESA. Margaret's not much for dancing, Tommy, you'll need to buy her a bun.

MARGARET. He'd need a coach full of buns and a unicorn pulling it before I'd want him hanging about. Go away, worm.

They're running off, laughing. THOMAS *hesitates then follows slowly.*

The Street, Prussia Street End, Evening

A few members of the Prussia Street gang enter and take up position on the bridge that marks the edge of their territory, peering down towards Bengal Street.

GEORGE *is at their head, looking down, staring down through the sunlit haze.*

JOE *walks up to him, walking through the gang. Other pedestrians are hurrying past, giving them a wide berth.*

JOE. You don't want to walk down there.

GEORGE *looks at him, instantly suspicious.*

GEORGE. You've talked to Susan.

JOE. No.

GEORGE. You have.

JOE. I can talk to Susan if I want to.

GEORGE. She don't want you, Joe. You look like a fool there.

JOE *trips* GEORGE *and pins him.*

JOE. Who looks like a fool now, Georgy?

GEORGE (*struggling*). I will fucking kill you, Joe.

JOE. Better men than you've tried that, squirt. Better and bigger.

GEORGE (*urgent*). Joe, serious, get off me. Get off me! They can't see me on the ground!

JOE *looks round and sees the rest of the Prussia Street gang. He lets* GEORGE *up.* GEORGE *whacks him, making him stagger.*

JOE. George!

GEORGE. Sorry, I'm sorry. They had to see me hit you, Joe.

JOE *starts to laugh.*

JOE. Only way you can hit me, George, if I let you.

GEORGE. I'll shake your hand now, alright?

JOE *doesn't do it right away, leaving* GEORGE *stranded with his hand out.*

Joe, come on.

Otherwise I'd have to stab you or something. You can't knock me over in front of everyone, Joe.

They shake.

JOE. I thought we were friends, you and me.

GEORGE. I'm not saying we're not, but you better never try that again.

What do you want?

JOE. Want to see what you're doing.

GEORGE. I'm just walking down the street. What are you doing?

JOE (*pointing*). Down that street? You're walking down that street?

GEORGE. I might. What's it to you?

JOE. Where does their territory start? Is it still the other side of the bridge there?

GEORGE. Until we push them back.

JOE. You still want to be a soldier, George?

GEORGE. No.

JOE. Last time I was here you were crazy to be a soldier.

GEORGE. Aye, well... I'm working now, in't I?

JOE. There's better places to do your fighting than Ancoats, if fighting's what you fancy.

GEORGE. No, don't want your fights, Joe. Your wars take years and you've nothing to show for it but gold ribbon. The night you first came stamping into The Mechanic like a platoon of infantry and blinded us all down with the light bouncing off your brass buttons I were only fifteen. Course I wanted to be a soldier.

It's good to see you, Joe, it's like a holiday seeing you back and hearing your stories again, but I think I'm making better money than you as it happens. And I know how to win a fight in Ancoats.

JOE. Know why I came in The Mechanic that night?

GEORGE. Best bar in Manchester.

JOE. No. Wanted to see if I could do it. Enemy territory.

GEORGE. What?

JOE. I used to run with the Tigers, never told you that but it's true.

GEORGE *doesn't believe him.*

No, it's true.

GEORGE (*still doesn't believe him*). When?

JOE. When I were younger than you.

GEORGE *is still just staring at him.*

I'm not joking.

GEORGE. No. You're not a Tiger.

JOE. But I was.

GEORGE. No, you're one of us!

JOE. I am now. Aye. I am since I met Susan... and you. I'm stopping, George, I've decided. I never wanted to come back, never wanted anything but to get away and be a soldier. But that baby's changed my mind for me. I'm stopping now and you're going to be my family.

GEORGE. That's not what she says.

JOE. Never mind what she says, I'm telling you how it's going to be.

GEORGE. Alright. So you can walk over the bridge with me.

On the other side of the bridge, SEAN, JIMMY, THOMAS, THERESA, POLLY and MARGARET are slowly gathering in a tight group, looking up at Prussia Street through the haze. JOE has seen them, GEORGE hasn't.

JOE. Not now.

GEORGE. Why not now?

JOE. Look.

Other members of the Tiger gang are gathering now, on this occasion they far outnumber the Prussia Street gang.

There's too many of them.

Don't step back, don't, hold your ground.

GEORGE *does so, nervous but facing down the Tigers.*

That's it. Just stand here. Stand here and let them see you.

GEORGE. How'd they get so many on the street this early?

JOE. Because the mills are stopped and no one's working.

From now on the two sides speak from their opposite ends of the street, occasionally overlapping each other.

SEAN (*peering*). Is it them?

THERESA. Can't make them out. I can see someone.

POLLY. There'll be hellfire any minute. From the ironworks. Then we'll see.

A flare of fire and the roar of the smelting furnace. It's halfway between the two gangs on Jersey Street.

JOE. That's lit us up. Now they can see us clear.

THERESA. Oh, the cheeky bastards. Oh, look at them!

SEAN. It is them, isn't it?

THERESA *is getting angry.*

THERESA. Just bloody standing there.

SEAN. I reckon they've been there a while.

MARGARET. What are they doing?

THERESA. Letting us know they're there.

GEORGE *is starting to enjoy the bravado.*

GEORGE. Look at them. Can't believe it, can they?

(*Shouting down.*) That's right, Tigers, we're coming for you. We are.

The Tigers are struggling to see through the hot haze.

SEAN. How many are there?

POLLY. Wait, wait till the hellfire comes again.

Another flare of flames somewhere in the smoke.

THERESA. I can't see their faces.

JIMMY. There's only two of them. We should just walk up there.

MARGARET. There's more further back, look. Who are they? I can't see.

JIMMY *has moved to the front of the Tigers, facing down the distant Prussia Street gang.*

JIMMY. We don't need to know their faces. We know who they are.

MARGARET. So who's that one? There at the front. He's in a uniform that one, see him? That's a uniform, isn't it?

JOE. Just stand here and give them a show.

JOE pulls out his sword and starts cleaning it deliberately.

SEAN. It's a fucking soldier. They've brought a fucking soldier with them.

GEORGE (*loving this*). Oh yes! Oh yes, watch out, Tigers, we'll slice you!

MARGARET. Is that a sword? Theresa, they're coming at us with swords!

JIMMY. Fuck that, I'll get a hammer to finish him off.

SEAN. Fuck that, my belt will do it.

MARGARET. They're standing there waiting. Look at them, they're just standing waiting for you to run at them.

SEAN. Not yet.

JIMMY. Why not yet!? Let's run at them! Come on!

JOE. They want you to start it.

THERESA. They want us to start it, but we won't.

JIMMY. Why the fuck shouldn't we?

GEORGE. Should we run at them then?

JOE. If you're ready for the fight.

GEORGE hesitates.

THERESA. We're ready but we're not just wanting a bit of slapping about on the bridge. We can get every Tiger in Ancoats out tonight, we can wipe them out.

GEORGE. Aye, we're ready. I'll show them ready.

He starts to stamp. A regular beat, behind him his gang join in. GEORGE takes a few steps forward, challenging. JOE closes up behind him.

JOE. Minute you step off the bridge you're in the fight. You want to do that now? I think there's too many of them. George? There's too many of them now.

GEORGE *looks back at his gang members. Their stamping grows in volume.* JIMMY *is enraged, he moves forward.* THERESA *follows.*

JIMMY. Tigers, will shut you up!

THERESA. Wait!

SEAN. Fucking get back here! We run at them when I say! When *I* say!

SEAN *pulls* JIMMY *back,* THERESA *is still standing further forward, staring.*

THERESA. Who is he? Who's the soldier?

The stamping grows louder, GEORGE *takes another step,* JIMMY *loses it.*

JIMMY. Run at them! Run!

JIMMY *starts to run full-pelt at the bridge.*

SEAN (*running too*). Oh, fuck it, Jimmy!

The others including THERESA *follow.* THOMAS *brings up the rear,* MARGARET *just watches.*

JOE. Fall back! They'll fucking kill you! Fall back!

He physically pulls GEORGE *back,* GEORGE *and the other Prussia Street gang members scatter.*

SEAN *and most of the Tigers stop but* THERESA *and* JIMMY *keep going.*

JOE *holds his sword and blocks their way.*

He's facing down THERESA. *She recognises him, he doesn't quite recognise her.* JIMMY *has stopped behind* THERESA, *intimidated by the sword.* THERESA *is on her own, staring at* JOE.

A frozen moment, then JOE *lowers the sword and turns quickly away.*

THERESA *is in shock.*

JIMMY (*shouting*). No! Fuck off back to Prussia Street. You can't take the Bengal Tigers! Not today! Not any day! We'll fucking tear you up!

SEAN *is pulling him back*.

SEAN. Shut your mouth, Jimmy! Just…! I call for the fucking fight! I do! Not you!

JIMMY. Then why aren't you calling for it?

SEAN. Because Theresa's right. We'll wait, we'll bring all the Tigers.

JIMMY. Oh, we do what Theresa says now, do we?

THERESA *walks slowly back to* MARGARET, *still shocked*.

MARGARET. What is it? Theresa?

JIMMY (*to* SEAN). Well, they're going. They've gone. They've vanished.

Back into the smoke.

Happy?

SEAN. Shut up, Jimmy.

JIMMY. That voice you're hearing? The one you want to shut up? That's your own self asking what you think you're playing at, asking if your courage just dropped out your arse.

SEAN. I say when we fight. I say.

JIMMY. So when are we fighting them?

SEAN. The Bengal Tigers are the best scuttlers in Ancoats, in all Manchester, even if there's only twenty of us on the street. But we don't fight unless I say we do. I think I need to teach you that lesson again, Jimmy.

SEAN *is taking off his belt*.

JIMMY *can't believe it*.

JIMMY. Are you fighting *me* now?

SEAN. Am I?

POLLY. Tigers don't fight Tigers.

SEAN. You want to say when we run, Jimmy, fight me first, then you'll have the right.

SEAN *whirls his belt in the air.*

POLLY. Tigers don't tear Tigers. Theresa? Theresa, stop them.

THERESA *doesn't react, still lost in her own shock.*

JIMMY. Fuck, Sean, that's not funny.

SEAN. No it's not.

JIMMY. No. No, I'm not going to fight you.

POLLY. Sean's king of the street, he earned it, in blood, we all saw him.

JIMMY. What are you? His talking monkey? Shut the fuck up.

SEAN. She's our tiger cub. She's our mascot. She just told you I'm king of the street.

JIMMY *looks round for support, doesn't see it.*

JIMMY. I know you are, I know.

SEAN. Good. Smack him, Poll.

POLLY *starts to giggle, moving in on* JIMMY.

JIMMY. What the fuck... get her away from me!

SEAN. Hey. I'm the king of the street and to prove it my little cub's going to smack you silly for cheeking me. Or do you want to fight me after all?

JIMMY (*quiet, furious*). No.

SEAN. On you go, Polly.

POLLY *slaps* JIMMY; *delighted, she slaps him again. He just takes it. She slaps him again.*

Alright, that's enough. Don't run at a fight again unless I'm telling you to and we'll stay friends, Jimmy. Alright?

SEAN *exits, followed by* POLLY *and other Tigers.*
MARGARET, THERESA, THOMAS *and* JIMMY *are left.*
JIMMY *hurt and angry, looking after* SEAN.

He sees them all watching him, goes for THOMAS.

JIMMY. What are you looking at? You're not a Tiger. You don't watch Tiger business.

THERESA. Leave him.

JIMMY (*turning on* THERESA). And you don't give me orders any more. Hear me?

THERESA. Whole street can hear you, Jimmy, you sound like a knob.

JIMMY *exits, angry.*

Sweet Christ I need a drink now and there's no work to pay for it.

THOMAS *holds up a silver coin.*

THOMAS. Jimmy's paying.

MARGARET. How'd you do that?

THOMAS. Fastest hands in Lancashire and he's too stupid to watch his pockets.

THERESA. So what are we waiting for?

The Street, Prussia Street End, Evening

SUSAN *is dressed for work, she's sitting on the wall of the bridge, soothing the baby.* GEORGE *is tying up her hair.*

SUSAN. Careful. Don't tug.

GEORGE. You're such a moaner. I don't tug.

SUSAN. No. You've got delicate hands for such an big ugly boy.

GEORGE. Shut up.

He pulls her hair gently.

SUSAN. You'll take him straight to Fran's.

GEORGE. It's too hot to keep him inside, I'll walk him up the street a bit first, let him breathe.

SUSAN. The air's dark and dirty. I don't want him breathing that.

GEORGE. He'll suffocate inside. I'll just cool him a bit.

SUSAN. And I don't want you on the street either.

GEORGE. What sort of trouble can a man who ties up ladies' hair get into? I'm too delicate for trouble, Susan.

SUSAN. So there's a bed at Fran's again now. That country girl? The one who never stopped crying for home? She just upped and left. Fran thinks she's taken off with some boy but I don't see it, she never stopped crying and who'd want that? I'm worried for her.

Still. She's gone.

More space than you've got where you are now. Cleaner too.

GEORGE. Me, back in a house full of women? I don't think so, Susan.

SUSAN. Alright. But I wouldn't bother you, I'd let you go your own way and...

GEORGE. No you wouldn't.

SUSAN. It's just 'cause I love you, George.

GEORGE. I know you do. Love you back. But I'm better living where I am.

SUSAN. Listen... I can't ask you to make me promises, I know that.

GEORGE. No, you can't.

SUSAN. But just promise me this.

GEORGE. What?

SUSAN. That you won't go chasing a fight.

GEORGE. You know what I think? I think you should give Joe a chance. Promise me you'll think about it.

SUSAN. That's none of your business, George.

GEORGE. See? You don't like it, do you? I won't do anything I don't have to. And I won't do anything while I'm carrying my nephew. I can promise you that.

All the rest... None of your business, Susan. I'm grown now.

SUSAN (*sighs*). Oh, you think so, do you.

She hands him the baby and walks down the street, moving into –

The Street, Night

The street is busier than ever. Some workers, like SUSAN, *are still moving through, most crowding round the pubs and bars.*

THERESA, POLLY, MARGARET, SEAN *and* THOMAS *are drinking in the street.*

JIMMY *watches nearby. He's moving amongst the other Tigers, talking quietly to one or two of them.*

SUSAN *makes her way unnoticed along the street and exits.*

Clogs banging on the street in the rhythm. Then THOMAS *is dancing, leading the dancers, taking the limelight. He pulls* THERESA *over to dance with him. She resists for a minute then she gets into it, whirling and stamping, laughing. Everyone's moving now.*

SEAN *moves in and takes* THERESA *out of the dance with* THOMAS.

SEAN. Don't you touch her.

THOMAS. I'm not, we're just dancing.

SEAN. No you're not, you're not dancing with her.

THOMAS. It's just dancing.

SEAN *has pulled* THERESA *away.*

THERESA. It's just dancing. He's better at it than you.

SEAN. Oh, you think? You think so?

SEAN *tries a move.* THERESA *laughs.*

THERESA. Aye, I do.

THOMAS *is just watching this, isolated again for a moment, then he is swept up in the other dancers.*

Lines of girls, arm in arm, process up the street in one direction. Lines of boys also linked walk in the other. When they collide, they jostle and scream and grab or grope at each other or run.

Every so often an older character edges through, almost all intimidated by the kids who've taken over the whole road.

One older MAN *pushes back as he's jostled.*

The dance breaks down as the young people push the MAN *out of their way,* THOMAS *is in this group.*

MAN. Oi! Watch it, you!

SEAN. Fuck off! Who're you pushing?

MAN. You don't own the fucking street, lad! Don't think you do.

SEAN. Who says we don't, who says!

(*Swinging his belt.*) You want a taste of this? Do you?!

They're all closing round the MAN *now, jostling and shoving him.* THOMAS *lifts the* MAN's *knife at this point but no one sees. The* MAN *breaks free, shouting back at them.*

MAN. Give it back! Give it back now!

SEAN. What? Lost something, have you?

SEAN *snatches the* MAN's *hat. The* MAN *goes to grab it back but thinks better of it as* POLLY *is squaring up to him too.*

MAN. Give me back my knife!

POLLY. You want to bring a knife on us? See what you'll get!

SEAN *slams his belt down. They're all shouting over each other.*

MAN. You all need locking up! The lot of you.

POLLY (*shouting over them both*). Tigers own Jersey Street. Tigers own the whole fucking street. You better believe we do!

They run at the MAN *and chase him off.* THERESA *snatches the hat from* SEAN *and puts it on.*

Never took his knife anyway, did you, Sean?

SEAN. Don't need his knife, I got this.

SEAN *whirls his belt again,* POLLY *joins in, they dance/play-fight, whirling their belts at each other and shouting.*

The other young men join in.

The young women advance on them again, stamping out a beat of their own.

The whole dance builds up again, they've taken over the whole road, up and down its length. Stamping and shouting. SEAN, POLLY *and all the other boys are slamming their belts down on the stones.*

Suddenly lights are going off. The dancers stop.

THERESA. What's going on? Are they calling time already? Margaret, they're closing up!

MARGARET. If there's no work there's no money for drink, is there?

THERESA. We got money!

(*Shouting at bar.*) Oi! It's not even midnight, I want a drink!

MARGARET. Oh fuck, Theresa. It's too hot. I'm *so* tired. Let's just get home.

THOMAS. I got a bottle. I got myself a bottle of gin.

He shows it inside his coat.

THERESA. Look at that. Quickest hands in Lancashire.

(*To* MARGARET.) He's got gin!

MARGARET. It's the middle of the night. I want *sleep*.

THERESA. Alright, alright. Come on, Polly.

POLLY *just shakes her head, she's watching* SEAN, *who's nearby talking to other Tigers.* JIMMY *has now moved over to join them.* SEAN *has seen* THERESA *making a move.*

SEAN. Where are you off to? We're having a war council here.

THERESA. What's to talk about? We'll run at them, tomorrow. Polly'll tell me when to be there.

SEAN. No, I want you here now.

He grabs her and kisses her. She allows it.

We'll make our plan. Then you're coming with me.

THERESA (*pulling away*). Am I fuck!

A stand-off.

MARGARET. You don't get it, do you? She chooses. Not you.

SEAN (*an announcement, a reminder*). I – am walking up Jersey Street tomorrow.

THERESA *moves closer to him again. Touches him.*

THERESA. And I'll be with you.

And after…

After we'll see. We'll see then.

She kisses him again and moves away.

SEAN. Alright.

He takes out chalk, talking to POLLY.

You know your job then? Like this.

He takes out chalk and scrawls a message quickly on the ground, just a 'tag', a symbol.

JIMMY. Are you worth it, Theresa, really? Are you worth it? What you got up your fanny that's so special?

MARGARET. You'll never know, you mangy little mill rat.

JIMMY. I wouldn't want to know.

MARGARET. You couldn't get your cock touched if you dipped it in treacle and left it out for the bees!

THERESA *is ignoring all of them, talking just to* THOMAS.

THERESA. Oi, man with the gin, you're with us.

(*As he hesitates.*) Where else are you going to sleep? The street?

He runs after her and MARGARET. SEAN *is watching this, frowning.*

JIMMY. Oh, look at that, Theresa's got herself a new pet.

POLLY (*to* SEAN). There's three of us in the bed most nights. I can watch them all night if you like. I can bite them if they try anything. I can, Sean…

SEAN (*cutting her off*). What you talking about? You just do the job I need you for and don't get caught. Go on. Hurry up.

POLLY *snatches up the chalk and runs off.* SEAN *throws chalk to other Tigers and they run in other directions, one of them pausing to tag the floor as he goes.*

JIMMY. That's it then.

SEAN. That's it.

JIMMY. Think we'll win?

SEAN. Tigers always win. Plus there's more of us than them. I just want broken heads, Jimmy, understand? A clean fight, nothing to get the peelers running about making trouble. Nothing any man will lose his job over. We'll cut them a bit, bruise them, send them home crying. Then back at work next week and all happy till the next fight.

JIMMY. You see… I don't give a fuck what the peelers do, Sean.

SEAN. Well… it's a good thing I'm leading the Tigers out and not you then, isn't it?

SEAN *exits,* JIMMY *snatches up chalk and scrawls a tag as he exits another way.*

The Street, Prussia Street End, Night

It's late, dark and quiet, but there are still people about, some slow pedestrians, going to and from work, some people sleeping on the street.

Others are watching, they are Prussia Street gang members on guard.

POLLY *comes flying over the bridge, she is chalking a big tag on the ground, the watching gang members see her.*

PRUSSIA STREET GANG MEMBER. Tigers! There's Tigers loose!

The Prussia Street gang members run at POLLY. *She just finishes the tag when they're on her. One of them has hold of her,* POLLY *manages to break free and flies back over the bridge.*

Another shout comes from the other side, distant.

VOICE (*shouting*). Tigers! Get them!

The gang members hesitate then run off on the direction of the new shout.

GEORGE *walks slowly up to the bridge, looking into the dark, down towards Jersey Street. He has the baby in his arms.*

JOE *comes up the dark street behind him.*

JOE. Thanks for this, George. Thanks, she barely let me see his face.

GEORGE *is holding the baby so he can see it.*

GEORGE. No doubt he's yours, ugly little monster.

JOE. Look at him! Look at him! He's wide awake!

GEORGE. Aye. Too hot to sleep. He never settles when it's hot like this.

JOE. He wanted to stay up to see his dad.

(*To baby.*) Didn't you? That's what it was, wasn't it?

GEORGE. Feel how thick the air is. There'll be a storm coming.

They're running all through Prussia Street territory. Must be coming up the canal.

JOE. That was how we used to do it.

(*He's still looking at the baby*.) Where is she?

GEORGE. At her work. She'll be at the dispensary all night. She doesn't mind me holding him, I'm his uncle.

JOE. What's his name?

GEORGE (*grins*). George.

JOE. Oh, you little fucker!

GEORGE. We're both named after my Uncle George really. Here.

He puts the baby in JOE*'s arms*.

JOE (*anxious*). Is he alright?

GEORGE. Course he's alright. He'll soon let you know if he's not, believe me, there'll be no doubt when he starts roaring.

JOE. He's heavy, heavy as a cannonball.

GEORGE. He's fat as one.

JOE. I'm asking you, George, have you ever seen a babe with legs like that? My boy's going to kick the world over when he's grown.

GEORGE. He's got a powerful kick, I'll give you that.

So. You've seen this?

He points out the tags.

JOE. Aye.

GEORGE. Looks like we'll have to kill all the Tigers tomorrow, Joe. Hope that won't upset you.

JOE. I told you. I'm here now.

GEORGE. Well… that's good, because I'll be leading the Prussia Street gang over the bridge tomorrow. The Tigers have called for a fight.

Beat.

JOE. How old are you now, George?

GEORGE. Sixteen.

JOE. How did you end up at the front of the Prussia Street mob?

GEORGE (*shrugs*). I won the fight.

JOE. Did you?

GEORGE. Yeah. With Harry Bold? Know him?

JOE. No.

GEORGE. Well, he were a knob, but he ran the Prussia Street gang. And he liked to push the little boys over, you know, be the big man. So I pushed back. And he were blind drunk. So I beat him. Easy.

Then I just had to front it out every time it needed fronting out. That was easy too.

JOE. Till now.

You worried you can't beat the Tigers?

GEORGE. We can wipe them out. There's hundreds of us, Joe. You haven't seen the Prussia Street boys for a while, have you? We've got two men for every Tiger. We can run them over.

JOE. So… what is it?

GEORGE *hesitates*.

GEORGE. I don't know how to do it. I don't know how to lead them out. I've never had to do that, see… How did you do it when you were a Tiger?

JOE. Just gave a good shout and started running. Don't look round to see if they're following, just keep running.

GEORGE. Right… alright… aye… easy…

JOE. You don't have to lead them out, George.

GEORGE. If I don't they'll say I'm a coward. They'll spit at me all down Prussia Street.

JOE. Are you sure you've got the numbers? Are you sure?

GEORGE. Aye. Two men for every Tiger, I promise you.

JOE. But they don't know that?

GEORGE. No, last time we fought the Tigers we were pitiful. We've three times those numbers now.

JOE. Then all you have to do is let them see that. Stand on this bridge and stamp. Let them see the army you've got. Let them hear it.

They can count heads.

There'll be some boy at the front of the Tigers even more scared than you are.

GEORGE. I'm not scared!

JOE. No shame in it, George. A fight's a frightening thing. So don't make one if you don't need to. Just don't make the move.

Let them run at you if they dare.

GEORGE. But they won't?

JOE. Well… if they do… two to one… you should beat them.

GEORGE. I'd have to be at the front, though. I've just never fought at the front, Joe. Not a whole mob.

JOE. You do what I've said, I'll be amazed if you need to. You won't need to fight this time, George. Just let them see you. That's all you'll have to do.

The baby starts to cry.

Aw fuck… what do I…?

GEORGE. Just jiggle him.

JOE *tries, clumsily. It's not working.* GEORGE *takes over.*

Give him here.

He takes the baby, quietens it expertly.

Will you walk down with us, Joe?

JOE. I promised Susan I'd keep you out of trouble, not take you out street-fighting.

GEORGE. Will you though?

JOE. I'll stand at the back, I'll be back there if you need me.

GEORGE. Thanks.

JOE. But you do what I say and you won't need me.

GEORGE. Thanks, Joe.

JOE. George, who was that girl? Running at us today?

GEORGE. What girl?

JOE. Running at the front of the Tigers?

GEORGE (*shrugs*). I don't know. Just some girl. Why? Did you know her?

JOE. I knew someone looked like her, but she wouldn't run with the Tigers, she were only a little thing, soft as a cotton ball.

GEORGE. Want me to find out?

JOE. No, no, leave it.

As they exit, a drunk is calling to GEORGE *from where he's sprawled in a doorway.*

He knows your name.

GEORGE. That's Harry Bold.

JOE. You're joking.

GEORGE. I'm not, that's the warning to us all, Joe, that's what happens when you lose a street-fight in Ancoats.

He throws the drunk a coin as they exit.

The Lodging House, Theresa's Bed

The room, the beds crowded round. The little light. THOMAS, THERESA *and* MARGARET *are all squashed together in the one bed.*

MARGARET *is trying to sleep.* THERESA *and* THOMAS *are drinking.*

THOMAS. Wait! Wait! Can you do this one, can you?

He pretends to take out his own eyeball, taking his time, grossing her out with the realism of the action then seems to push his eye at her.

(*Horrible creepy old-man voice.*) I've got my eye on you, young lady.

THERESA (*laughing and disgusted*). No! Stop it! Get him off me!

MARGARET. Fuck's sake! I'm trying to sleep!

THERESA. What do you need to sleep for? There's no work tomorrow, is there?

MARGARET *sits up then.*

MARGARET. How can you not be worrying about that? We shouldn't even be out drinking. When will we ever get money again? The mills are quiet. No one's working. No one knows if there'll ever be any thread again. How can you not be frightened?

THERESA (*to* THOMAS, *fake solemn*). She's right, Thomas. There's no thread in the looms. Empty looms. Did you ever think of anything more terrifying than that?

THOMAS. How about two hundred Tigers running through the streets?

THERESA *slaps at him in delight.*

THERESA. Now that's frightening!

They both fall about laughing.

Don't mind Margaret. She's scared of everything.

MARGARET. I'm not!

THERESA (*still to* THOMAS). She's my little chick, my clueless little chick, she fell out the nest going 'cheep, cheep, cheep' and I picked her up, didn't I, little chick?

MARGARET *says nothing*.

Oh, look at that face? What's wrong, little chick? You worried you won't have any corn to peck tomorrow? I'll feed you.

THOMAS. We'll get her a seed cake.

THOMAS *and* THERESA *fall about*.

MARGARET. It's too hot. The air's too thick to breathe. I want the storm to come. I want my sleep. Are you going to be drinking all night?

THOMAS. What if we are?

THERESA (*to* THOMAS). No, you shut up now.

(*To* MARGARET.) You're upset. What are you upset about?

MARGARET. What happened to what you said?

THERESA. What?

MARGARET. You said there'd never be anyone in my bed again I didn't want.

THERESA. Well, he's not stopping!

THOMAS. Oh, thanks.

THERESA. God, look at the state of you! Your face is tripping you! Stop being so scared the whole time, Margaret! It's boring me now.

MARGARET. I'm not scared.

THERESA. You are, but you need to stop it. You can't be scared of the likes of him!

THOMAS. Hey! I'm dangerous!

THERESA (*still just to* MARGARET). Listen now, I told you how it is. You're with me now. I'll look after you. I know you can't even speak above a whisper and you'd fall over without me holding you up but I will hold you up. You've just got to remember that. That's all you have to do, so stop your fussing.

MARGARET. I can speak.

THERESA. Aw, Jesus. Margaret...

MARGARET. I can stand up myself...

THERESA. Margaret, you're so brainless you thought your mum's boyfriend only climbed in your bed because he was feeling a draught in hers.

THOMAS *is laughing at this.*

MARGARET. Don't talk to him about that.

THERESA. I'm not! I'm talking to you!

MARGARET. I don't want him here.

THERESA. Well, this is my bed, I pay for it, I've put this roof over your head and this blanket over you and he's got gin. That's it!

A voice speaks up angrily from the darkness.

VOICE. Oh, for fuck's sake! Drink your gin and go to sleep!

THOMAS *and* THERESA *both turn on the noise. They speak together.*

THERESA/THOMAS. Shut up!

THOMAS. Shut up or we'll bottle you!

MARGARET *gets up and exits, fast and angry.*

THERESA (*calling after her*). Margaret! Margaret!

THOMAS. What's up with her?

THERESA. I don't know. She gets moody sometimes. She had the stupidest mother in Manchester and the shame of it sends her moody sometimes.

THOMAS. Oh no, my mum were stupider than hers, guarantee it.

THERESA. You think?

THOMAS. I know.

They're making a game of this now.

THERESA. No, no, I think you'll find my mother was actually stupider than yours.

THOMAS. I'll drink to it...

(*He does so and passes her the bottle.*) But I'm telling you my mum's stupider than that.

POLLY *runs on, breathless.*

POLLY. Where's Sean?

THERESA. Somewhere else.

POLLY. He's going to love me. Know what I did? I even climbed up and got the Tigers chalked up on the pub sign for The Mechanic! Can you believe it? Our mark swinging outside their pub. Where's he want me to go now?

THERESA. I don't know! Find him and ask him!

POLLY *starts to move off.*

POLLY. Where's Margaret?

THERESA. She fell in the canal and drowned.

(*As* POLLY *hesitates.*) I don't fucking know, Poll. Go if you're going, we're drinking here.

POLLY *exits as* THERESA *swigs more gin.*

Right, this is how stupid my mother was. You've no idea. She were that stupid. Know what she did?

THOMAS. What?

THERESA. She left me and my big brother with four. Four! Like a basket of kittens. Four! 'Just feed them,' she says, 'You know how to do that.' Then she's off!

THOMAS. Four what?

THERESA. And they were stupider than her. Easy to know they're hers. A kitten has the sense to come running when you've food for it, but did they? No. Did they have the sense not to fall in ditches or under a cart? No.

THOMAS. She gave you a bag of cats?

THERESA. She might as well have done. I were only ten. My
    brother was fourteen… What did she think would happen?
    'Just keep hold of them all,' she says. How was I supposed to
    do that? They were all running about already.

THOMAS. Kittens are mad.

THERESA. My sisters, you idiot! I'm talking about my sisters!

THOMAS. She left you with your sisters to look after?

THERESA. Aye.

    Well, what did she think would happen?

THOMAS. Where did she go off to? Your mother?

THERESA. Well, she died, didn't she? Haven't you been
    listening?

THOMAS. Your mother died?

THERESA. Haven't you been listening?

THOMAS. What did she die of?

THERESA. I don't know. She were just sick. I tried to look
    after her. We'd no money for a doctor with her too sick to
    work. She pulled me to her and her hands were that hot and
    her breath smelled like a drain but I loved her. I did.

    Her face was that thin at the end but I thought she was
    beautiful because I knew it was the last I'd see of her. I was
    holding on to her hot hands, tight, tight because I knew she
    was going, I was begging her not to up and die and leave me
    but I knew she couldn't help it really. She weren't stupid
    then. She was sick. But that was the last thing she said to me,
    'Just hold on to your sisters.' Now that were stupid because
    how could I do that? She died saying a stupid thing like that
    and it tore me to scraps.

THOMAS. So where's your brother?

THERESA. Well, *he* wasn't stupid. He ran off. Ran off and left
    me to look after her mess.

THOMAS. So where are your sisters?

THERESA. They all got sick. Like her.

THOMAS. Are any of them living?

THERESA. Mary Ellen might be in the workhouse in Oldham. I'll get over and look one day. She were the littlest. I doubt I'd know her now if I fell over her.

They tore her out my arms.

I could've held on to her. Maybe. They should have let me try. There was only me though, I couldn't hold them.

They all slipped away from me like water through my hands, like warm blood going cold as it leaked out of me.

Mary Ellen could run faster than me, she could. You should have seen her! Like a little beetle, scuttle across a room faster than you could throw a shoe.

THOMAS. I ran. I ran all the way to Ancoats.

THERESA. What for?

THOMAS. Because this is my place.

My mother, my mother was so stupid… she was so stupid she couldn't have another kid without she had to find a split new dad for it.

She couldn't remember my dad at all. One day she's telling me he was working on the railway. The next she told me he'd gone up north…

I don't think she liked my dad. I think she'd forgotten him altogether and then she saw him on my face and started remembering.

So whatever she remembered it must have made her angry…

So this one day I've thrown a stone at John the joiner next door. Not a big rock or anything, just a pebble, just for the fun of seeing him jump a bit, you know?

He says, 'Why don't you go and break windows and scuttle folk in Ancoats like your dad and leave decent folk their peace.'

And she took his side over mine.

And my big sister says she doesn't care if I never come home.

And my big brother never says a thing, just gives her half his wage and goes out like he's king of the house.

When I said I was going the only person that cried was my little sister.

I miss my little sister Martha.

She's good at the reading.

I were never good at reading. All the letters dance about, like they're playing a trick on me.

THERESA. Was he really from here? Your dad?

THOMAS. He were the king of the street. Thomas Clayton.

THERESA. I've not heard of him.

THOMAS. That's 'cause it were back in olden times. Long ago. But I know.

THERESA. How do you know?

THOMAS. Well, why else would I have ended up here? I followed his name to Ancoats.

That's the only thing I'm sure of. 'I should never have given you his name,' she says, 'even his name's trouble.'

It's powerful trouble my name. I'm sure of that.

She should have loved me best. I were the only one of us that could dance.

She likely loved Martha best. You always love the littlest best, don't you?

THERESA. But your brother's working?

THOMAS. They're all working 'cept little Martha. Mum has a laundry business, you know? We had half the house, just for us.

THERESA. Thomas, you could go home.

THOMAS. No.

THERESA. You could.

THOMAS. Not till I'm somebody. Not till I can show her.

I'll be king of the street soon. You'll see. I'll be rich soon.
I'll be able to look after you.

THERESA. There's no one looks after me but me, and I look
after everyone else, that's how it is. Couldn't keep those
kittens alive but I keep the pets I have now.

THOMAS. What happened to your brother?

THERESA. Went to be a soldier.

He ran off when the first of them got sick. He never looked
back. I thought he might be dead.

THOMAS. He's not?

THERESA. No, he's not.

THOMAS. Where is he then?

THERESA. Prussia Street.

THOMAS. What?!

THERESA. Aye. I saw him. On that bridge. Clear as anything.
Joe the soldier, waving his fucking sword.

THOMAS. That was your brother?!

THERESA. Or his ghost.

THOMAS. Did he recognise you?

THERESA. Didn't seem to.

Fucker.

Still hasn't got the courage to walk down Bengal Street, has
he?

THOMAS. He lived here?

THERESA. Oh aye.

THOMAS. And now he's standing up there?

THERESA. Aye.

THOMAS. Oh, the fucking Judas! The fucking turncoat!

THERESA. That's my big brother. Right enough he should be scared to come back here. I would kill him. I'll watch the Tigers do it now.

Give me the gin.

She grabs it and swigs.

I'm glad he's come back. I'm glad I'll get to see him die.

THOMAS. The Tigers will tear him! They'll…

THERESA (*cuts him off*). You're five minutes here and all the rest of your life in Chorlton. Shout about the Tigers when you've tried running at the front.

THOMAS. I will. You watch me.

THERESA. They'd kill you. I don't want to see you die. I want to see him die. That's what has to happen.

She drinks again. THOMAS *moves closer. He takes the bottle off her.*

THOMAS. Do you want me to kill him for you?

THERESA. You're not a fighter.

THOMAS. No?

THERESA. No, you're a dancer, remember? Think you'd be stopping here if you were a fighter?

THOMAS. Am I stopping here then?

THERESA. There's no one left to throw you out and I'm too tired now. You can sleep at the bottom there till Polly gets back.

THOMAS. I'd rather be up here, with you.

THERESA. I bet you would. Fuck off down there or I will kick you out altogether.

He takes the knife out and shows her.

THOMAS. I'll put this between us.

THERESA. Where'd you get that?

THOMAS. I told you. Fastest hands in Lancashire.

This'll protect you. Of course, if it's not there I can just lean over and do this.

He kisses her. Puts the knife between them.

But if the knife's there.

He leans close but stops before he kisses her, very close.

See? I can't reach you unless you take the knife away. You're protected.

THERESA. Am I?

THOMAS. Unless you want me to take the knife away.

A beat.

THERESA. No. Leave it where it is. For now.

THOMAS. Suit yourself.

But I could do anything you asked, you know.

THERESA. Oh, they all say that.

THOMAS. But when Thomas Clayton says a thing he means it. That's what his name means. So remember it.

THERESA. Alright, Tommy.

THOMAS. Thomas.

THERESA. Thomas.

THOMAS. That's better.

He settles down to sleep. There's a thunder in the dark. Feet stamping on the cobbles.

(*Half-awake.*) What's that?

THERESA *laughs.*

THERESA. Listen to them. It's the Prussia Street mob, letting us know they got the message, letting us know they're ready.

THOMAS. Christ… Sounds like an army.

THERESA. Doesn't matter how many there are, Tigers will eat them all.

They stamp again.

THOMAS. No… they can't make as much noise as the mills. That's just a lullaby, that is.

THOMAS *is drifting off to sleep. The noise grows louder. Perhaps the Prussia Street mob can now be seen, stamping round the little light and* THOMAS *and* THERESA. *Whatever happens we get the sense of them drawing closer, closing in.*

THERESA *gets up carefully, leaving* THOMAS *sleeping. She faces the noise. She puts the light out.*

Darkness. Silence.

ACT TWO

The Street, Night

THOMAS *stands alone on the quiet street, the half-drunk bottle of gin in his hand. He's looking round for* THERESA.

THOMAS (*calling*). Theresa?

(*Louder.*) Theresa!

He listens to the silence for a moment.

(*To himself.*) Too hot. Too quiet.

He moves off as JIMMY *and a few Tigers prowl up the street. It's darker. They are somehow more threatening than we've ever seen them, the few pedestrians are terrorised. Some break into a run.*

JIMMY *and the Tigers hiss at them and frighten them but they're waiting for something else.*

POLLY *walks through on her way home.* JIMMY *calls her over, quietly.*

JIMMY. Hey... hey... Sean wants you. And the other two.

POLLY. He told me to get off home when I was done.

JIMMY. Well, now he wants to see you. And your friends.

POLLY. Theresa won't come, she's told him. And I don't know where Margaret is.

JIMMY. Are you Sean's little tiger cub or aren't you? I've told you his orders.

POLLY. Well, tell him I'll look for Margaret. That's the best I can do. You can't order Theresa.

POLLY *runs off.*

*There's distant stamping, the Prussia Street fighters getting
ready again.*

JIMMY *and the Tigers stamp back.*

Then they scatter into the dark.

The Ancoats Dispensary

*Beds crowded close together, all full, coughs and occasional
quiet groans.* MARGARET *is on an empty bed, sitting on it,
waiting.* SUSAN *is in her nurse's apron, checking patients
nearby.*

MARGARET. I'm not stopping if I've got to wait this long.

SUSAN. That's up to you.

MARGARET. It's just my ear. It's just my ear's sore. That
won't be serious, will it?

SUSAN. Can't tell without looking at it.

MARGARET. Well, are you going to look at it?

SUSAN. In a minute. It's three in the morning. I'd've thought
earache could wait till dawn.

MARGARET *is looking around.*

MARGARET. I like it here.

SUSAN. Do you?

MARGARET. Aye. It's clean.

SUSAN. Well, you wouldn't like the job of keeping it that way.

MARGARET. Yes I would.

SUSAN *looks at her.*

I love cleaning, me.

MARGARET *gets off the bed, looking around.*

You got a mop?

SUSAN *just points*. MARGARET *goes and gets it. She starts mopping the floor, humming to herself.*

In't it quiet without the engines going?

SUSAN. Yes.

MARGARET. Why are all the people quiet in here?

SUSAN. They're not breathing too well.

MARGARET. Likely they'll die.

SUSAN. Nothing wrong with their hearing though.

MARGARET. Sorry.

(*Speaks closer to one of the bodies in the beds*.) Sorry, missus. Likely you won't. I'm so tired I wouldn't know sense if it bit my arse and held on till I sat on it. It's the gin talking.

(*To* SUSAN.) Where's all the doctors then?

SUSAN. Sleeping. One'll be along soon.

MARGARET. How come you're not sleeping?

SUSAN. Because I'm working. When did you last sleep?

MARGARET. I was tired but I'm waking up now. I'm doing a good job on your floor here.

SUSAN. You should sleep. You'll not be safe to work if you haven't slept.

MARGARET. Do it all the time. You'd never get any dancing at all if you worried about that.

SUSAN. You'll fall in the machine.

MARGARET. Not me. Anyway, no one's working tomorrow. Look how lovely I'm making your floor, missus.

SUSAN. It's good.

MARGARET. In't it though? I love work, me. Work like this.

SUSAN. Like what?

MARGARET. Making things better.

Cleaner.

SUSAN *looks at her for a moment, considering.*

SUSAN. Can you read?

MARGARET. Do I look stupid?

SUSAN. That's the first job of a nurse. Making things clean. That's the most important part of the job at the end of the day, I reckon. For the rest you need to be able to read.

MARGARET. What do you read?

SUSAN. The doctor's notes.

Course, this job don't pay as well as the mills.

MARGARET. Quieter though.

SUSAN. Aye. And there's always work. Never run out of sick people. I'm keeping two on what I make.

Leave that, let's have a look at your ear.

MARGARET *sits on the bed.* SUSAN *comes and looks.*

Wait till I get a light on you.

(*Holds a lamp or candle near* MARGARET's *ear.*) Nice and still, please.

MARGARET. You smell nice.

SUSAN. Thank you.

MARGARET. Is it soap?

SUSAN. Probably.

SUSAN *turns away to get instruments.* MARGARET *sees them.*

MARGARET. Oh, you're not getting near me with those!

SUSAN. Don't be silly. I won't hurt you.

MARGARET (*warning*). I can bite!

SUSAN (*ignoring that*). Nice and still again, please.

She *lifts something out of* MARGARET's *ear and stares at it, fascinated.* MARGARET *looks.*

MARGARET. Oh, sweet fucking *Christ*!

Sorry. I'm sorry. Didn't mean to swear all over you.

Aw, Jesus! Look at it! Look at it!

SUSAN. You had a miracle in your ear.

She's examining it, opening it out.

MARGARET. It's a beetle! There was a beetle in my ear! Aw, Christ, I had a beetle in my ear!!!

SUSAN. It's not a beetle.

MARGARET. Don't tell me that! I can see its legs!! Oh, it's not alive, is it! Tell me it's not alive!

SUSAN. No. It's quite dead, poor thing.

MARGARET. Poor thing. *Poor thing!* It was probably going to burrow in and eat my brain! Look at it! It's all greasy and dirty and disgusting…

SUSAN. It's a butterfly.

MARGARET. It's not.

SUSAN. Look.

She's opened out its wings so MARGARET *can see.*

MARGARET. It's blue.

SUSAN. It's beautiful.

MARGARET. How did it get in my ear?

SUSAN. I don't know. Do you sleep with your window open?

MARGARET. There's no window in the room I sleep in.

SUSAN. It must have got lost.

MARGARET. I suppose.

SUSAN. Got lost and thought your ear was a flower.

MARGARET. Has it hurt me?

SUSAN. No. It just died, quietly, in your ear. Must have been quiet or you'd've felt it moving. I'll wash it out for you.

MARGARET. Scrub it!

SUSAN. No, your ears are delicate.

MARGARET. My ears?

SUSAN. Anyone's ears.

> SUSAN *is busying herself cleaning* MARGARET*'s ear gently.*

MARGARET. How do they work?

SUSAN. What?

MARGARET. Ears? Where's the bit that makes you hear? Is it inside?

SUSAN. You have to be very careful not to poke anything in too far. You could damage your hearing.

MARGARET. What's in there?

SUSAN. Tiny, tiny little bones. Smaller than bird bones.

MARGARET. Butterfly bones.

SUSAN. Maybe.

MARGARET. How do you know that?

SUSAN. The doctor showed me.

MARGARET. Are there ear doctors? Is that a real thing?

SUSAN. Not here.

> (*Finishes.*) There. All clean.

MARGARET. What will you do with the butterfly?

SUSAN. It's your butterfly. It chose you.

MARGARET. I wish it hadn't!

SUSAN. I'll show it to the doctor. Then I'll pin it on a card. As a curiosity.

> How old are you?

MARGARET. I'm sixteen.

SUSAN. You could work here.

MARGARET. No.

SUSAN. I started working here at sixteen.

MARGARET. I couldn't do that.

SUSAN. Why not? You can keep things clean.

MARGARET. Yes, but…

SUSAN. What?

MARGARET. I'm not fit for something like that. I couldn't talk to a doctor.

SUSAN. Oh, they do all the talking. Don't you worry about that. And why couldn't you?

MARGARET. Doesn't sound like something I'd do.

SUSAN. How do you know what you'd do? You had a butterfly in your ear and you didn't even know. The world's full of wonders.

I could ask the doctor. You could work a few days. See how you get on. We need another nurse badly but there's not many like the work.

MARGARET *hesitates*.

MARGARET. I don't know. I'll finish mopping your floor, though.

MARGARET *goes to start cleaning again*.

SUSAN (*amused*). What, you'll do the work before you take the job?

MARGARET. It's calming me, this. Helps me think.

SUSAN. Well, don't let me stop you.

MARGARET. I can't sleep when it's hot like this. Makes my head thump. There's a storm in my head. But this is sweeping it out of there. I'll finish this and get off.

SUSAN. Sleep here for a couple of hours. It's not safe out there.

MARGARET. No?

SUSAN. There's trouble out there.

MARGARET. What trouble?

SUSAN. Like you don't know. Maybe one of your Tigers has found out I'm from Prussia Street, from the other side of the bridge.

MARGARET. Are you?

SUSAN. Plenty people walk up and down for work all the time but they're looking for people like me tonight. Looking for anyone they can bite. You'd best stop here till daylight.

Unseen by either of them, POLLY *has entered under this. She speaks now, startling them both.*

POLLY. She doesn't have to worry about the Tigers. We don't eat our own.

SUSAN. Are you sick?

POLLY. No.

SUSAN. Then get out of here. You're making the floor dirty.

POLLY. And you don't just live up on Prussia Street, you're George William's sister, your brother is king of Prussia Street.

SUSAN. My brother is a fool of a boy that doesn't have the sense to stay away from the likes of you, but I'm teaching him. So you stay away from him.

POLLY. We'll slice him if he puts one toe on the stones of our street. We'll slice you too.

SUSAN. And then who'll sew your head up when it's broken, little girl?

POLLY *is abruptly furious.*

POLLY (*roaring*). I ain't a little girl!

One of the sick people in the beds wakes, groaning horribly, scaring MARGARET *and* POLLY.

SUSAN *quickly soothes the patient.*

SUSAN. Keep your voice down, will you.

POLLY (*quiet*). I'm a tiger cub and I could bite your throat out if I wanted to.

SUSAN. Good for you. What do you want?

POLLY *points at* MARGARET.

POLLY. I came for you. I was sent. Sean wants you.

MARGARET. No he doesn't. It'll be Theresa he wants.

POLLY. He said to get you too.

MARGARET. What for?

POLLY. I don't know but you'd better come quick, hadn't you?

POLLY*'s already moving out.* MARGARET *hands the mop back to* SUSAN.

MARGARET. I'm sorry.

SUSAN. You can still stop here if you want. I've looked inside your head, remember. No Tigers in there.

MARGARET. No. I need to go.

SUSAN. Up to you. Come back if you think you want that job, though.

MARGARET. No. I couldn't do what you do. I'm scared of sick people.

She follows POLLY.

The Street, Night

POLLY *and* MARGARET *are slowly surrounded by* JIMMY *and a few other Tigers*.

POLLY. Where's Sean?

JIMMY. What do you want him for?

POLLY. I don't know. What does he want us for?

JIMMY. That's what I want to know.

MARGARET *is reading the situation, seeing the threat*.

MARGARET. Polly, let's get home.

JIMMY. You'll run around and do anything if you think Sean wants it done, won't you? Why's that then?

MARGARET. Polly, come away.

POLLY. Because he's king of the Tigers.

MARGARET. Polly...

JIMMY. Well, some of us think it's time there was a new king. Someone who doesn't wait to start the fights, someone who doesn't let the likes of you and her and your friend Theresa run with the Tigers.

POLLY. I've been a Tiger since my teeth grew through my gums. Who're you to tell me what I can do?

JIMMY. You're not getting this, are you, little monkey? I'm the new king of Bengal Street.

The gang members move in on the girls. MARGARET *makes a run for it*.

MARGARET. Polly, run!

MARGARET *gets away.* POLLY *is surrounded.* THOMAS *enters and watches*.

POLLY. You touch me, I'll bite you. You touch me, Sean'll open you up.

JIMMY. We wouldn't hurt you, little tiger cub. You're our mascot, aren't you? You can still be with the Tigers, little

Polly. We'll still have a use for you. You just need to learn to dress right.

JIMMY *holds up a lurid dress.* POLLY *realises what he means.*

POLLY. Don't you fucking dare… don't you…

They pounce on her, trying to tear her clothes off. POLLY *is fighting and screaming.*

She manages to break free and runs but crashes into THOMAS.

JIMMY. Get her!

THOMAS *is startled but he holds on to* POLLY *as she struggles.* JIMMY *and the others grab her and pull her off into the dark.*

THOMAS *is left gaping after them.*

POLLY *screams again, more distant.*

THOMAS. Shit.

The Street, Prussia Street End, Night

THERESA *stands just on the edge of Prussia Street territory, looking up. She hears* POLLY *screaming in the dark behind her.*

She looks round.

When she looks back, JOE *is standing on the bridge.*

JOE. It is you.

THERESA. Yes.

JOE. I thought if it was you you'd have to walk back up for another look. You never could rest if there was something you wanted to find out. And you never could sleep when it was hot like this. Not since you were a baby. I saw you coming up the street. I thought it had to be you.

THERESA. Well done. You remember me.

JOE. And you remembered me. You recognised me.

THERESA. I can't forget your face, Joe. Every man I've ever kicked bloody has had your face.

JOE. Oh, don't talk like that. When did you start kicking anyone? When did you start running with the Tigers? I don't like that.

THERESA. Don't you?

JOE. Aren't you glad to see me again?

THERESA *says nothing*.

I'm coming back to live here, Theresa. I've got family here now. I don't want there to be trouble between us.

THERESA. Then stay that side of the bridge. Because if you come over here you're dead. The Tigers will tear you. You know they will. You remember.

JOE. No. There'll be no fighting now.

How're the girls? How did they turn out?

THERESA. What do you care?

JOE. Course I care. How are they?

THERESA. They were already sick when you left. Didn't care then, did you?

JOE. Tell me they got better.

THERESA. No.

JOE (*shock*). Are they dead?

THERESA. Yes.

JOE. No. No, Theresa, I didn't... I never thought of them dying...

I didn't know what to do, Theresa. I couldn't feed all of us.

THERESA. You could have done better than me.

A beat.

JOE. I've got a son now.

THERESA. Good for you.

JOE. That makes you an auntie now.

THERESA. You can invite me to the christening then.

JOE. Maybe we will.

THERESA *makes a scornful noise.*

Say something to me, Theresa. I'm glad to see you. I am.

THERESA. Are you a good soldier, Joe? You've got a medal, on your chest there, what's that for?

JOE. My whole platoon got them. It's nothing.

THERESA. No. What was it for?

JOE. Courage. Under fire.

THERESA. Is that right? Didn't see that in you six years ago. Let's see how you do tomorrow.

JOE. There won't be any fighting tomorrow. They've got two men to every one of you. Tell your boys to back off.

THERESA. I'll tell them to run at you till they've run you all down.

JOE. Theresa. Tell them, they're outnumbered.

THERESA *doesn't respond.*

Fuck's sake, Theresa, I was barely fourteen! I was a boy!

She turns at that.

THERESA. Older than me.

She stares him down for a moment. He starts to walk off the bridge.

Stay off Tiger land, I'll kill you myself.

THOMAS *is shouting behind her.*

THOMAS. Theresa! Theresa!

THERESA (*to* JOE). Hear that, Joe, Tigers are coming. Run, Joe. Run.

>JOE *turns and walks slowly away as* THOMAS *runs to* THERESA.

THOMAS. They got Polly.

THERESA. Who did?

THOMAS. Just come.

The Street, Dawn

POLLY *is crumpled in the street, she's bruised and bleeding. She's wearing the lurid dress, it's torn, half-hanging off her.*

THERESA *comes on first, she stops dead, staring at* POLLY *in horror.*

THERESA. Jesus… Poll…

>POLLY *can't speak, breathless with pain and shock.*

>THOMAS *follows* THERESA. *They just look at* POLLY.

POLLY. Don't look at me. Don't let him look at me.

>THERESA *turns on* THOMAS.

THERESA. Why didn't you stop them? You ran?

THOMAS. I ran to find you!

THERESA. You *ran*!?

THOMAS. There were ten of them!

THERESA. You coward! You just stood and watched them do that to a little girl…?!

THOMAS. No!

POLLY. I ain't a little girl!

MARGARET *hurries on, bringing* SEAN *and other Tigers.*
They too stop in horror.

SEAN. Who did it? Who?

JIMMY *walks out of the shadows with his supporters behind*
him.

JIMMY. I don't like being slapped, Sean. You should know that.

For a moment no one speaks. POLLY *staggers to her feet.*

POLLY (*to* JIMMY). Give me my clothes back.

(*To* SEAN.) Make him give me my clothes back.

Still no one speaks.

You can stop looking at me like that. No one fucked me,
alright. No one.

They never touched me. They just... I just need my clothes
back.

SEAN *is looking at* JIMMY.

SEAN. Did you touch her?

JIMMY. No.

MARGARET. No, but you'd have tried with me or Theresa,
wouldn't you, if you'd caught us.

JIMMY. Wouldn't, just wanted to slap you about. Like he had
me slapped.

SEAN. Polly? Did any of them touch you?

POLLY. They hurt me.

SEAN. But did they...?

POLLY (*cutting him off*). No! I fucking told you! No! Make
him give me my clothes back!

JIMMY. Sean, she can't be running at the front, like she's a real
Tiger, look at her. Look at the state of her. Tigers in
petticoats? You're making us a joke. You should have seen
that. Seen how it made you look.

And we should be running up at Prussia Street, not waiting for them to run at us.

And we shouldn't be worrying about what the peelers might do. We rule these streets, not them.

SEAN. Is that what you think?

JIMMY. Yes, that's what I think.

SEAN. Well, I suppose we need to fight for it then.

THERESA. We don't have time for this. It's getting light. Prussia Street is coming.

JIMMY. And I'm fucking *tired* of listening to her tell us who we should tear and who we shouldn't, and when we should run and when we shouldn't...

SEAN. Thing is, Jimmy, she talks sense, you just talk.

All this while SEAN *and* JIMMY *are taking off their belts, getting ready to fight.*

JIMMY. And I've my Tigers with me now so we'll see who's talking when we're done.

THERESA. The daylight's here. Prussia Street have been getting ready all night. They're coming.

SEAN. Well, they can wait on this, it needs doing...

POLLY. Make him give me my clothes!

SEAN. Be quiet, Polly. You can't be a Tiger any more.

POLLY. No! Sean, please! *Please!*

SEAN. Shut up, Polly. You shouldn't be a tiger cub. You're too big now. He's right.

JIMMY. I'm right, am I?

SEAN. One thing you're not right about though.

JIMMY. What's that?

SEAN. You'll never be king of Bengal Street.

They start fighting, whirling their belts at each other, a balletic deadly duel of whirling buckles.

*As they fight, the stamping starts from Prussia Street,
growing closer and closer.*

THERESA *turns to watch, waiting to see.*

Everyone else stays absorbed in the fight.

*For a while it's just a whirl of flashing belts, dodging bodies,
each man evading the other's blows. Then* SEAN *gets two
blows in quick succession.* JIMMY *cries out, dropping to his
knees, clutching his face, bleeding.* SEAN *stands over him.*

So who leads the Tigers, Jimmy?

JIMMY (*hurt, breathless*). You do.

SEAN. Everyone agree with that?

He looks round, reading the answer.

*The stamping is getting louder, louder, closer. Then it stops
abruptly. The Prussia Street gang appear at the other end
of the street, on the other side of the bridge.* GEORGE *is at
the front.*

They stand, waiting.

There are twice as many of them as there are Tigers.

JIMMY. Jesus, look at them all.

SEAN. There's too many of them.

JIMMY. What do we do?

JOE *has walked up to stand behind* GEORGE. THERESA *is
staring at him.*

THERESA. We run at them.

SEAN. There's too many of them.

MARGARET. Look at the clouds. A storm's coming. It's going
to break.

THERESA. We're the storm. We'll break over them.

SEAN. There's too many of them, we can't run at them. We
can't.

THERESA. We have to!

JIMMY. We can't.

MARGARET. They can't do it, Theresa, they'd get cut to pieces.

THERESA. We have to! Polly!

POLLY (*dull*). You heard him. I'm not even a Tiger any more.

THERESA. God, you're worms! The lot of you! *Worms!* We're the Bengal Tigers! We can beat anyone. We're the fiercest scuttlers in Manchester!

SEAN. Face them, boys. Face them but fall back.

The Tigers are starting to do that, backing off in formation behind SEAN, *who still faces* GEORGE *and the Prussia Street gang.*

Thunder rumbles.

THERESA. Do none of you care what I think of you!?

Do none of you care if you look like cowards!?

Is there not one of you cares if anyone even remembers your name!?

If we don't fight now, when will we fight at all!? *Come on!*

SEAN *and the rest of them are still backing off.*

Then THOMAS *steps out of the ranks of Tigers, walking forwards, walking towards the Prussia Street gang.*

Thunder rumbles.

GEORGE *looks round at* JOE, *uncertain.*

GEORGE. What do I do? Joe? Do we run at him? What do I do?

JOE *hesitates.*

THOMAS *is gathering speed. He takes out the knife, raises it.*

Oh, Jesus!

THERESA. Tear him, Thomas!

The storm breaks. THOMAS *is on* GEORGE, *lightning-fast,
he kicks* GEORGE's *feet out from under him and stabs him
as he falls. The other members of the Prussia Street gang fall
back, shocked at the sight of the knife.* JOE *moves quickly up
to face* THOMAS.

THOMAS *holds the knife high in the air, threatening* JOE,
who is momentarily too shocked to react. THOMAS *plunges
the knife into* JOE's *chest.*

*The fight has turned completely. All the Prussia Street mob
turn and run and the Tigers roar after them, chasing them
out and off.* SEAN *is at their head.*

JIMMY *and* SEAN *have closed on* GEORGE, *beating at
him with boots and belts where he lies on the ground.*

THOMAS *just stands, watching* JOE *staggering then
crawling.* THOMAS *walks after* JOE, *bends and stabs* JOE
*in the back. He raises his bloody knife high as he runs after
the other Tigers, yelling.*

MARGARET *and* POLLY *are left with the wounded,*
GEORGE *and* JOE.

MARGARET. Aw, Jesus… Polly… we have to… we have to…

Polly, we have to get them to the dispensary!

POLLY *is ignoring her, tearing off the tatters of dress she's
wearing.*

POLLY. You do what you like. You should have got me my
clothes back. That's what you should have done.

MARGARET. Polly! Help me!

POLLY. I don't have to help any of you. I'm not a Tiger any
more. I'm going to fuck the lot of you.

Very upright and dignified in her underclothes, POLLY
walks past the wounded men and exits.

MARGARET *runs to* JOE *and* GEORGE, *bending over
them, shouting.*

MARGARET. Help me! Somebody help me!

A couple of the Tigers come back on, confused and a little shocked. They watch MARGARET *as she struggles to lift* GEORGE, *then finally they come to help.*

They carry the young men into –

The Dispensary

SUSAN *is working on another patient. She looks round, startled as they enter.*

MARGARET. Help them. You have to help them.

SUSAN *moves closer. She recognises* GEORGE *and* JOE. *It hits her like a blow.*

SUSAN. No… no… no…

MARGARET. What do we do? How do we help them?

SUSAN. Oh, dear God… oh, sweet Jesus… no…

MARGARET (*shaking her*). Help them.

SUSAN. We have to stop the bleeding. We have to… Put them on the table! Quick! Put them there!

The young men lift GEORGE *and* JOE *onto an examination table.*

SUSAN *is hurrying now, getting bandages.*

You have to help me.

MARGARET. Yes.

SUSAN. We have to stop the bleeding.

MARGARET. Tell me what to do.

SUSAN *is faltering again, trying to make a decision.*

SUSAN. Oh, God help me, I don't know which of them… I can…

(*Shouts at the young men watching*.) Run to get the doctor!
Quick. He'll be at the infirmary. Tell them there's boys dying
in Ancoats!

She grabs MARGARET*'s hands and a wad of bandage. She
forces* MARGARET*'s hands onto* GEORGE*'s wound.*

Hold that. Hold that down tight, *tight*. Don't you let go. Not
for anything.

She starts working on JOE.

MARGARET. It's moving, under my hand.

SUSAN. That's his blood, that's his heart. You feel that stop,
you shout. You shout the minute you feel that.

MARGARET (*wonder*). I'm holding his heart.

SUSAN *is bending over* JOE.

SUSAN. Joe? Can you hear me?

He wakes a little.

You're alright. You're in the dispensary. The doctor's coming.

JOE. Susan.

SUSAN. Yes.

JOE. Did I hit my head?

SUSAN. You got stabbed, Joe.

JOE. Did I? Little fucker. Christ, yeah, hit me like a horse
trampling me. I remember. Am I bleeding much?

SUSAN. I think so. Yes.

JOE. I can't see it.

SUSAN. It's on the inside, Joe.

JOE. That's alright then, that's where blood's supposed to be,
on the inside.

SUSAN. We need to stop you bleeding, Joe.

She's working on him as they talk.

JOE. So I was thinking, what you said, I can borrow a horse, the sergeant will let me. I thought I could give you a day out.

SUSAN. Did you?

JOE. Yes. Because I reckon you need that and I could give that to you. We could go out to the fields together. Let baby George feel the grass under his toes, let his feet feel clean running water for the first time. That'd be a good thing, wouldn't it? We could take a picnic.

SUSAN. Yes.

JOE. Because you need that. You need sunshine and clean air, both of you.

SUSAN. Yes.

JOE. So there you are. That's something you need and I'll give it to you.

SUSAN. Alright.

JOE. So will you marry me now?

SUSAN. Keep asking me.

He's slipping away.

Joe, keep talking to me.

Joe.

Joe.

He's gone.

Other Tigers are drifting in now, some of them are injured or bloodstained, SEAN, JIMMY, THERESA, *watching, shocked, silent.*

SUSAN *is bent over* JOE *for a minute, overcome.*

MARGARET. Susan? Is that your name?

SUSAN (*quiet*). Yes. What?

MARGARET. I can still feel it. It's still strong.

SUSAN. What?

MARGARET. His heart. I can still feel it.

SUSAN. Good. That's good.

Then we need to sew him up.

MARGARET. Like mending a blanket?

SUSAN. Just like that. I'll need you to hold where I tell you while I do it.

Just for a moment she almost loses it. She kisses JOE *then she gets it together. She's getting the equipment she needs. She turns to* GEORGE *and starts work.*

THOMAS *enters and watches too.*

MARGARET. I think I could work here.

SUSAN. Good. Watch what I'm doing so you can do it another time.

POLLY *enters. She's wearing a* POLICEMAN*'s jacket, way too big for her. Two* POLICEMEN *are following her.*

POLICEMAN (*to* SUSAN). What have you got, Susan?

SUSAN (*working*). A stabbing. And a murder.

The POLICEMAN *looks at* POLLY*. She points at* SEAN *and then* JIMMY*.*

POLLY. Him and him.

The other POLICEMAN *moves on* SEAN *and* JIMMY*.*

JIMMY. You fucking *Judas*!

POLLY. Should have given me my clothes back.

SEAN *and* JIMMY *are taken off.*

POLICEMAN. Anyone else?

POLLY *looks at* THERESA*.*

POLLY. No.

POLICEMAN. You didn't see who did the stabbing?

POLLY *looks at* THOMAS*.*

POLLY. No. Just some nobody.

POLICEMAN. What?

POLLY. Some nobody from nowhere. He's not even a proper
Tiger. Can't even think of his name.

THOMAS. Thomas Clayton.

THERESA. Thomas, shut up!

POLLY. I don't even know why he was there. I could be
looking right at him and not tell you what he was called.
He's nobody.

THOMAS. Thomas Clayton.

POLLY. He's not a Tiger. I was a Tiger from when I first could
run at all and never saw him before last week. I'm more a
Tiger than he'll ever be. He's nothing.

THOMAS. I'm Thomas Clayton and you'll all remember what
I did.

POLICEMAN. So he did the stabbing, is that what you're
saying?

POLLY. Some nobody like him did.

THOMAS. I did!

THERESA. Jesus! Thomas!

POLICEMAN. Well, that's good enough for now.

He moves on THOMAS.

THERESA. You can't come back to my bed, Polly.

POLLY. Don't want to. When I'm fifteen I can start as a
policewoman. They get a uniform. They get a stick. I know
where you all sleep and I'll come back and hit all of you
with that stick. You wait.

POLLY *follows the* POLICEMAN *off.*

SUSAN (*still working on* GEORGE). Now the rest of you go
away and leave us in peace.

They all exit except THERESA. *She's looking at* JOE.

THERESA. I want to sit with him.

SUSAN. No.

THERESA. Please. I knew him. I want to sit with him.

SUSAN. You knew him? How did you know him?

THERESA. This is my brother. Joe.

SUSAN. Is it?

THERESA. Yes.

   He walked over that bridge to Prussia Street six years ago
   and he never walked back till tonight but he's my brother.

SUSAN. He should have stayed in Bengal Street.

THERESA. He should never have come back.

   A beat.

SUSAN. You can sit with him till I'm done here. Then you can
   help me lay him out. We'll talk after that if we've strength
   for it.

   THERESA *sits by* JOE *as* SUSAN *and* MARGARET *go on
   working.*

   At the same time we see –

A Prison Cell

The POLICEMAN *is pushing in* JIMMY, SEAN *and*
THOMAS.

JIMMY. Sergeant, I need…

POLICEMAN (*cutting him off*). Nothing till morning now, lads.
   Just hold on to it.

   The POLICEMAN *closes the door on* THOMAS, JIMMY
   and SEAN.

SEAN. You stuck it to him, Tommy.

THOMAS. Thomas! Get my name right, will you!

SEAN. Sorry.

THOMAS. Should have killed him with the first blow.
Shouldn't have needed two. He was asking for it though.

JIMMY. He was.

SEAN. He got what was coming to him.

THOMAS. Next time.

My dad showed me how to stab a man in the heart. He were
the best fighter. He was a king in a street-fight. A king. You
remember his name.

JIMMY. No.

THOMAS. You do because I told you.

SEAN. Did you?

THOMAS. He were the king of Ancoats. The king.

Maybe they hung him. That's where he went. They'd think
he was too dangerous to walk about, he'd've killed a
policeman just by stamping his foot and breathing on him.

SEAN. I thought you said you'd never seen your dad. I
remember you saying that.

THOMAS. I know who he was.

JIMMY. Well, how did he show you how to stab a man in the
heart if you never met him?

THOMAS. Are you calling me a liar?

JIMMY. Never that.

THOMAS (*finds a thought*). He left me a letter.

SEAN. Did he though?

THOMAS *turns on him, threatening*.

Sorry, Thomas. I don't mean anything. Tell us about the letter.

Throughout this, the dispensary is disappearing. It transforms back to the street, a few pedestrians straggling through.

Still in her police coat, POLLY *stands by the place where* JOE *fell, looking at the blood on the street.*

THOMAS. My mother read it to me. When I left her. She was crying and begging me to stay. But I wouldn't, so she read his letter to me, he told me I was his son and I had to make him proud. And Mum said she knew then I had to go. I had to come and be king of Ancoats. Like him.

JIMMY. You're the king tonight.

SEAN. Aye, you're the king.

On the Street

POLLY *stops someone walking up the street who's about to walk through the blood.*

POLLY. Don't walk there. A man died there. That's a man's blood.

In the Prison

THOMAS. I should have stabbed him in the heart. I will next time.

THOMAS *is shaking with tension and adrenaline.*

Cold in here. Why's it so cold in here? We're like three sides of beef hanging in the butcher's.

JIMMY. Have my coat, Thomas.

THOMAS *hesitates.*

JIMMY. Go on. I'm not cold. You should have it.

THOMAS. Alright.

He lets JIMMY *give him his coat.*

Thanks.

On the Street

POLLY *stops someone else.*

POLLY. Don't walk there. A man died there. That's a man's blood.

In the Prison

SEAN. Will they hang you? Do you think they'll hang you?

THOMAS. Makes no difference. Makes no difference to me. As long as they remember my name.

There's a distant rumble. The mills starting up again.

JIMMY. Listen. The mills are working again.

The sound grows and grows.

The police cell disappears completely into –

The Street, Day

The mills grow in volume. The street throngs with people again. They move to the rhythm of the street, the rhythm of their work.

POLLY *is still trying to protect the blood, shouting now, but she's barely audible above the sound of the mills.*

POLLY. Don't walk there. A man died there. That's a man's blood!

The crowd sweeps over her, carrying her off.

The sound and movement grow faster, build up and up, then…

Darkness.

Silence.